W9-CBH-817

FOLLOWERS OF THE
North Star

Rhymes about
African American Heroes,
Heroines, and Historical Times

SUSAN ALTMAN AND
SUSAN LECHNER

Illustrated by Byron Wooden

CHILDRENS PRESS®
CHICAGO

Since the beginning of time, slavery has existed. In 1619 it was introduced into Jamestown, Virginia, then a British colony in North America. By 1641 Massachusetts had legalized it, and other colonies soon followed. Although slavery existed throughout colonial America, it became an important economic institution in the South where a large labor force was needed to harvest sugar, tobacco, and cotton.

In America, there always was resistance to slavery. Each year thousands of slaves ran away in search of freedom in the northern United States and Canada. Slowly they made their way across mountains and rivers, through swamps and forests. Often they were forced to hide during the day and travel only at night in order to escape detection. These runaway slaves didn't have compasses or roadmaps. They couldn't risk stopping along the way to ask directions. Instead, they relied on natural signs, such as the stars, to guide them. Of special importance was the North Star, also known as Polaris, which is part of the Little Dipper constellation. This star appears almost directly in line with our North Pole. For this reason, thousands of runaway slaves followed it as they fled north.

The early followers of the North Star were people of tremendous courage. If caught trying to escape, they were severely punished. Some were even killed. Still they persisted in their dream to gain their freedom. It is in respect for these courageous people, and the thousands of other African Americans who have followed their dreams to create a better life for themselves and others, that we have named this book.

CONTENTS

FOLLOWERS OF THE NORTH STAR

Like early slaves who followed
The North Star's guiding light,
To free themselves from bondage
And gain what was their right,
Their children's children's children
Grew up to join the fray,
And battle for the freedoms
That we enjoy today.

Some struggled for the right to vote,
An end to segregation,
A chance to work at any job
Or gain an education.
In struggle never ending,
They strove for Liberty,
Justice, Truth, and Equal Rights,
And human dignity.

Like early slaves who followed
The North Star's guiding light,
We follow in the path they made
In search of what is right.

EXTRAORDINARY ◆ AFRICAN ◆ AMERICANS

CRISPUS ATTUCKS
1723-1770
American Patriot

In early U.S. history
When we were just a colony,
British soldiers stood around
Creating trouble in the town
  Of Boston.

The colonists saw one solution —
We've got to have a revolution!
Independence! That's our goal!
And Crispus Attucks played his role
  In Boston.

The air was cold that winter's day.
The wind blew from the south.
A young boy, maybe
Twelve years old,
Was shooting off his mouth.
He showed a soldier disrespect.
The soldier said, "I'll break your neck!
Don't think that you can talk like that!"
And then he gave that boy a whack!
Was 'bout to kick him, but he ran,
And that is how it all began
  In Boston.

Well, people started getting mad
Because the boy was crying.
They grabbed some snow
That packed real well,
And snowballs started flying.
Then somebody picked up a rock
And threw it at the guards.
The soldiers yelled, "OK, that's it!"
And ran out in the yard.
The soldiers stopped and raised their guns,
Then the crowd began to run
    In Boston.

But Crispus Attucks stood his ground.
He said, "They can't push us around.
Knock 'em over!
Make 'em pay!
Don't let them treat us in this way!"
The angry crowd took up the cry.
The soldiers fired, and Attucks died
    In Boston.

Called "The Boston Massacre,"
It changed things from the way they were —
Everywhere.

JAMES ARMISTEAD
1760-1832
American revolutionary war spy

A black man from Virginia,
Whose name was Armistead,
Helped win our revolution
When we were almost dead.
Assigned to help out Lafayette,
He came up with a plan
To infiltrate the British camp
And trick their high command.

It seems their chief, Cornwallis,
Was searching for an aide
To keep him looking as he should
When passing in parade.
"Here's the deal," said Armistead,
"I know my etiquette.
I'll get that job and soon send back
Reports to Lafayette."

"This is great!" said Lafayette.
"These last months have been rough.
The Brits control Virginia, and
My men have had it tough.
Now I can start to plan my raids
To catch the British snoozing.
With spy reports from Armistead,
We'll win; we won't be losing!"

But then the British disappeared!
Ol' "Laf" looked like a geek!
"Check Yorktown out," said Armistead,
"It's by the Chesapeake."
He passed the word to Lafayette
Who got there just in time.
The fate of thirteen colonies
Was really on the line.

"Laf" joined up with G. Washington
And French Admiral DeGrasse.
Soon General Cornwallis
Was cut off at the pass.
We won the fight at Yorktown,
The British said no more.
And now the work of Armistead
Is part of battle lore.

BENJAMIN BANNEKER
1731-1806
Mathematician, astronomer

Though twelve before he started school,
Ben Banneker was no one's fool.
His grandma gave him his first book,
And, honey, that was all it took.
He read whatever he could get,
Though comic books were not out yet.

And then at night, when Ben got done,
He'd do arithmetic for fun!
Ninety-nine times thirty-three,
He'd get the answer instantly!
Six trillion times two-forty-eight,
You'd never even have to wait.

Ben also carved a wooden clock.
You think that's easy? Well, it's not!
We're talking tiny wheels and gears.
It ran, they say, for forty years!
You must admit, that's quite a claim.
Can your alarm clock do the same?

And then Ben wrote an almanac,
Which told the most amazing facts
Of stars and rain, and roots and berries,
Of how to grow delicious cherries.
How to rid a dog of fleas,
What to do for knobby knees,
Where to find a gunny sack —
It's all there in Ben's almanac!

While Ben was working up a sweat,
Our congressmen began to fret.
"We are," they said, "in great distress.
We need a place to meet the press;
Engage in furious debate;
And comment on affairs of state;
Where we can be both wise and witty;
In fact, we need a whole new city!"

And so Ben got a letter from
The famous Thomas Jefferson.
(You've heard of him — delightful fellow —
He used to live at Monticello.)
Tom wrote, "Dear Ben, We're on our knees!
If you could only help us please!
There is this Frenchman named Pierre,
Smooth and suave and debonaire.

"To get down to the nitty-gritty,
We've asked him to design a city.
And Pierre (last name L'Enfant)
Said 'Sure, guys, anything you want.'
But he can't do it by himself.
We think Pierre could use your help.
Our brand new city needs your touch.
We're short on cash; don't charge too much!"

Ben wrote and said, "No need to plead,
I know exactly what you need —
A place with lovely boulevards,
Shopping malls, and neat trimmed yards,
Monuments and galleries,
Stuff that tourists like to see;
Where folks can meet the president
And stage inaugural events.
We'll name the city Washington
To honor George for all he's done."

But when they started out to work
Pierre turned out to be a jerk.
He threw a fit — went back to France
With D.C.'s plans still in his pants!
Congress cried, "What will we do?
The plans are gone — the money too!
Critics clamor for inspection.
This could cost us reelection!"

Ben Banneker stood up and said,
"Don't worry, boys. It's in my head.
The plans for Washington D.C. —
I'll recreate 'em. Count on me.
Just need a couple days to think.
I'll have 'em for you in a wink.
The extra work will be for free
Because it's under warranty."

And that is how it all got done —
Our capital at Washington,
A city with wide boulevards,
Shopping malls, and neat trimmed yards,
Monuments and galleries,
Stuff that tourists like to see,
Where folks can meet the president
And stage inaugural events.
So come and visit, check the view,
Benjamin Banneker made it come true!

HARRIET TUBMAN
1821-1913
Abolitionist/Underground Railroad conductor

Harriet Tubman,
Courageous and brave,
Escaped from her owner
Who'd held her a slave.

But she was determined
To make all blacks free,
And made nineteen trips South
To help others flee.

Slaveholders muttered and put up their posters.
"Wanted, alive or dead!"
A large reward was publicly offered
For Harriet Tubman's head.

But Harriet Tubman was smarter than they were.
She knew what had to be done.
And three hundred slaves were brought out to freedom
On her Underground Railroad run.

Before they would leave, she'd get them together,
And tell them they couldn't turn back.
Once they got started, they'd head north for freedom
On the Underground Railroad track.

Harriet Tubman,
Courageous and brave,
Never forgot
She'd once been a slave.
Harriet Tubman
Pierced slavery's wall.
This woman called "Moses"
Now honored by all.

ESCAPED SLAVE

Running, running, got to get away,
Travel by night, hide by day.
Dogs on my trail, men with guns,
Nowhere to rest, keep on the run!

Get away, get away,
Got to get away.
Keep on running, find a way.
North Star guide me,
Don't let them find me.
Woods and marsh and twisting track,
Road so muddy,
Feet all bloody,
Keep on running,
Can't turn back.

Running, running, got to get away.
Travel by night, hide by day.
Dogs on my trail, men with guns,
Nowhere to rest, stay on the run!

Get away, get away.
Got to get away.
Nowhere safe for me to stay.
Run from the whips and
Chains and beatings,
Endless hours in blazing sun.
Hunger, sorrow,
Hopeless tomorrows,
Can take no more,
Got to run.

Running, running, got to get away.
Travel by night, hide by day.
Dreams of freedom, liberty,
No more bondage, got to be free.

BLACK CIVIL WAR SOLDIERS
1861-1865

Two hundred thousand black men
Fought in the Civil War.
And thousands died
Amid the cry
Of "SLAVERY, NO MORE!"

DEADWOOD DICK

(Nat Love)
1854-1921
Cowboy and range rider

This African American cowboy
Was one you'd like to know.
He could ride.
He could rope.
He could stalk antelope
And play a guitar with his toe!

A rodeo rider,
A bronco buster,
A sure-shot shooter was he.
A lariat legend,
An outlaw hunter,
With a horse named "Fricassee."

This African American cowboy
Could wrestle and punch and kick.
He could scout.
He could trail,
Catch a bull by the tail,
And his name was DEADWOOD DICK!

BUFFALO SOLDIERS
1870s-1890s
The black cavalry

Buffalo, buffalo,
Buffalo soldiers,
Riding tall and proud.
Buffalo, buffalo,
Buffalo soldiers,
Dark as a thundercloud.

Protecting settlers
And pioneers
From outlaws and rustlers and more,
These brave black troops
Helped lead the way West
After the Civil War.

The Indians called them
Buffalo troops
For their hair was curly and black.
Like buffalo
They were fearless and strong
And courageous under attack.

Of the cavalrymen
Who rode the range
They ranked among the best —
The famous buffalo soldiers
Who helped to change the West.

Buffalo, buffalo,
Buffalo, buffalo,
Buffalo, buffalo,
Buffalo soldier.

Buffalo, buffalo,
Buffalo, buffalo,
Buffalo, buffalo,
Buffalo soldier.

Whoa!

GARRETT MORGAN
1865-1963
Inventor

Explosions ripped through tunnel five,
Killing many men.
Rescuers could not get through.
There was no oxygen.

Gas and smoke and deadly fumes
Filled tunnel number five.
As minutes passed, the chance grew less
Of finding men alive.

"Call Garrett Morgan," someone said,
"He's worked on this invention!"
"A gas mask? Will it really work?"
They asked with apprehension.

In darkness Morgan entered,
Searching everywhere,
His gas mask strapped across his face
To purify his air.

Back into that killer mine,
Again and then again,
Till Morgan rescued thirty-two
Of the unconscious men.

Later during World War I,
The gas mask gained new fame.
It saved the lives of thousands
Who never knew his name.

- GARRETT MORGAN -

GRANVILLE T. WOODS
1856–1910
Inventor of electro-mechanical devices

They called him "The Black Edison"
Because of all the work he'd done—

Inventing things mechanical
For use on jobs industrial,

A third rail that's electrified
So crucial for a subway ride,

Equipment that the railroads lack
Preventing problems on the track—

With sixty major patents won,
It's Granville Woods, "Black Edison."

GEORGE WASHINGTON CARVER

1861-1943
Botanist and agricultural chemist

George Washington Carver was so clever.
Farming methods changed forever.
At Dr. Carver's instigation
Farmers learned of crop rotation.
And then he showed them what to do
With all the excess crops they grew.

> From common plants,
> And weeds, and soil,
> He made fine woodstains,
> Cheese, and oil,
>
> Butter, starches,
> Rugs, and glue,
> Vinegar, and
> New shampoo,
>
> Synthetic rubber,
> Things to drink,
> Tapioca,
> Printer's ink.
>
> Insulation,
> Paint, and rope,
> Paper, flour,
> Dyes, and soap.

George Washington Carver was so clever.
His name will be enshrined forever.
This son of slaves showed us the way
To make the most of every day.

Now you can follow in his path
By learning sciences and math.
Then maybe someday when you're grown,
You'll make discoveries of your own.

INK

MATTHEW HENSON

1866-1955
Explorer

Matthew Henson
Pursued a special goal.
He and Robert Peary
Discovered the North Pole.
  You have to be a hero
  When it's sixty below zero,
And freezing blasts of arctic winds
Can take a savage toll.

Matthew Henson
Loaded up his sled.
He and Robert Peary
Made plans to trudge ahead.
  Though ice froze on their clothes,
  And frost attacked their toes,
They reached their destination, and
The news began to spread.

What happened after that
Was a monumental shame.
Though Henson got there first,
Reporters never gave his name.
  But the world now knows the story.
  Henson has his share of glory.
And we honor Matthew Henson
With his rightful claim to fame.

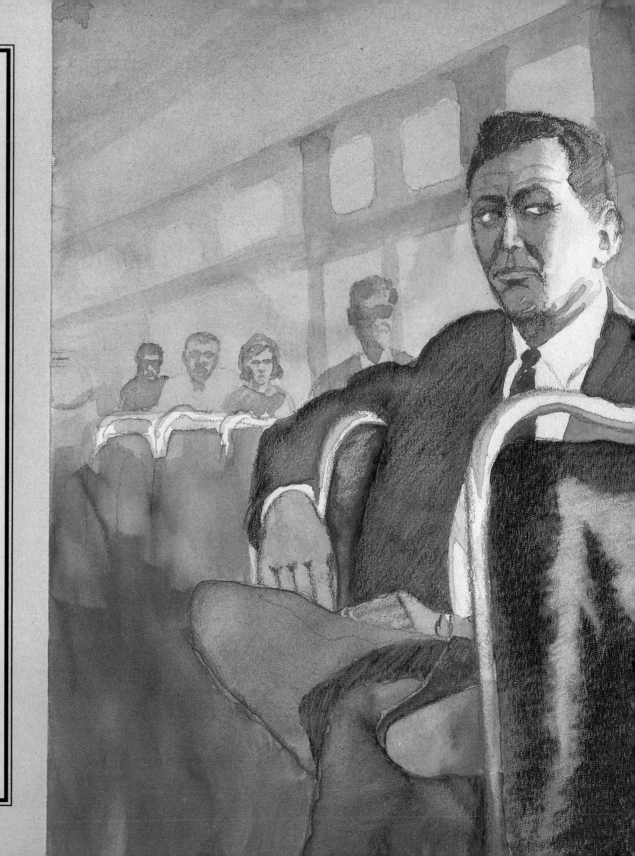

ROSA PARKS
1913
***Her opposition to bus segregation
led to the Montgomery Bus Boycott***

Montgomery, Alabama,
In 1955 —
Ms. Rosa Parks had finished work.
"I'm going home," she cried.
"I'm going to see my husband.
I'm going to watch TV.
I'm going to put my feet up,
'Cause I'm tired as can be."

The bus pulled up.
She paid her fare
And wearily sat down.
She didn't know
She was about
To turn things upside down.

The bus driver,
He looked around
And gave a nasty stare.
"That seat is just for whites," he said,
"You know you can't sit there."
Well, Rosa Parks,
She stared right back.
She said "It isn't right
That the seat where I am sitting
Is set aside for whites."

"I'll call the cops," the driver said —
A mean look on his face.
"Call 'em," Rosa Parks replied.
"I'm staying in this place."

They came and took Ms. Rosa Parks
Away into the jail.
She had to telephone a friend
So she could get her bail.

Her neighbors said,
"That's it, we're through!
We say enough's enough.
We want our rights
To any seat.
We're tired of this stuff."

They said, "A boycott's what we need.
That bus system will pay.
Till we can sit just where we want,
We all will stay away.
We'll walk,
We'll jog,
We'll roller skate,
We'll run,
We'll even crawl.
Till we can sit in any seat,
We just won't ride at all."

The boycott lasted one whole year
'Cause nobody would ride.
The bus owner
Was real upset.
I think he even cried.
"OK, OK, OK," he said.
"I'm sorry. Please come back.
From now on it's first come, first pick
For riders white or black."

Now all of us
Sit where we choose.
There aren't any fights.
'Cause Rosa Parks sat down that day,
And stood up for our rights!

JACKIE ROBINSON
1919-1972
First black major league
baseball player

For many years,
Across the nation,
Baseball upheld
Segregation.

Black men couldn't
Make their mark
At Wrigley Field
Or Fenway Park.

The Brooklyn Dodgers
Changed all that
When they signed Robinson
To bat.

He hit 'em low.
He hit 'em high.
He made that baseball
Really fly!

With Robinson
On second base,
The Dodgers moved
Up to first place.

He scored the runs,
Was MVP,
And led the team
To victory.

With Brooklyn's Dodgers
(Now L.A.)
He paved the way
For blacks to play.

'Cause segregation
Is not fair
In baseball, school,
Or anywhere.

And Robinson made millions shout
When he struck
Segregation out.

THE LITTLE ROCK NINE

*First black students to integrate
an all-white high school in
Little Rock, Arkansas, 1957*

The mob formed early—
A danger sign.
State troopers were set
In a menacing line
To block the path of
"The Little Rock Nine."

Nine young black teens,
First day of school,
Faced threats, and slurs,
And ridicule.
But even so,
They kept their cool.

"Lynch 'em! Kill 'em! Hang 'em high!
Keep them out of Central High."

While most folks watched it on TV,
The White House said, "This will not be!"

"We won't be stopped by racist groups.
We're going to send in paratroops!"

And so amid the hue and cry,
The soldiers came to Central High.

They stayed all year in that morass
To walk those nine black kids to class.

> Elizabeth Eckford,
> Minniejean Brown,
> Terrance Roberts
> Stood their ground.

> Melba Pattilo,
> Ernest Green,
> Thelma Mothershed
> Stayed serene.

> Gloria Ray,
> Carlotta Walls,
> Jefferson Thomas —
> Heroes all!

SIT-INS

Part of the Civil Rights Movement
Greensboro, North Carolina, 1960

"WE DO NOT SERVE NEGROES!"
Said the signs around town.
You can buy. You can pay.
But you cannot sit down.

You can take food outside;
But you'll never be able
To sit at the snack bar
Or eat at a table.

UNTIL . . .
Four students from college
Sat down to be served.
They were firm, but polite,
And would not be deterred.

Though threatened and spat on,
They came back each day,
With more and more friends,
All demanding fair play.

WHITE·ONL

AND SOON . . .
All over the country
The "sit-ins" just spread.
Whites joined in with blacks,
And they forged on ahead.

There were "kneel-ins" at churches
And "swim-ins" at pools,
"Read-ins" and "pray-ins"
Demanding new rules.

AT LAST . . .
These courageous young people
Woke up the whole nation.
Soon Congress was calling for
New legislation.

Those students who "sat-in"
With true dedication
Taught us a lesson
And smashed segregation.

MEDGAR EVERS
1925-1963
Civil rights activist

Shot down beside his own
    front door,
Shot because he'd take
    no more.
Resolved to vote as was
    his right,
To rectify the
    black man's plight,
To crush injustice,
    bigotry,
Discrimination,
    poverty.
They shot him by his own
    front door,
But could not kill what
    he stood for.

GIVE US AMERICAN RIGHTS

GO HOME NEGRO

MALCOLM X
1925-1965
Minister and civil rights leader

X marks the spot
Where he stood firm
And spoke with forceful voice
Of those not seen —
   Defamed,
   Demeaned —
Denied an equal choice.

X marks the spot
Where he condemned
Robed killers in the night,
Shielded by lies —
   Uncaught,
   Untried —
Consumed by hate and spite.

X marks the man
Who spoke for all
Whom bigotry rejects,
With head unbowed —
   Defiant,
   Proud —
This man called Malcolm X.

LEONTYNE PRICE
1927
Opera star

Symphonic,
Harmonic,
Melodic,
Dramatic,
Fantastic,
Electric,
Leontyne Price!

Magical,
Rhythmical,
Lyrical,
Classical,
Musical
Miracle,
Leontyne Price!

LORRAINE HANSBERRY
1930-1965
Playwright

She was barely in her twenties,
And her life had just begun
When she wrote a moving play
She called A RAISIN IN THE SUN.

Her tale about a black family
Made audiences cheer.
The Broadway critics voted it
The "Best Play of the Year."

In languages around the world,
They translated her text.
It soon became a movie;
Then a musical was next.

Spotlights,
Opening nights,
She had a ball!

Movie rights,
Neon lights,
She had it all!

Then illness struck Ms. Hansberry.
Too soon, her life was done.
But we still have her legacy —
A RAISIN IN THE SUN.

MARTIN LUTHER KING, JR.
1929-1968
Minister, author, and civil rights leader

They tried to kill the Dream
When they shot down Dr. King.
But the Dream he preached remains alive
In spite of everything.

The Dream of equal justice,
Of freedom, liberty,
The Dream that all the world can live
As one community.

In spite of all the hatred,
Suspicion, rage, and strife,
The Dream is there for all who seek
To find a better life.

Though Martin Luther King is dead,
The Dream he preached lives still
In hearts of all good people,
And there it always will.

THE DREAM

LIVES

ARTHUR MITCHELL
1934
Founder of The Dance Theatre of Harlem

Arthur Mitchell didn't care
When people said that blacks
Could never dance ballet because
They lacked the proper backs.
Their bodies just were not shaped right,
Their feet, too wide or flat.
"Oh, they can tap, or break," folks said,
"But nothing more than that."

Well, Arthur Mitchell worked and trained,
Then leapt onto the stage.
Ballet fans cheered — the critics raved.
It was a whole new age!
He soared right to the very top.
His name was really hot.
Then came that day in '68
When Dr. King was shot.

He asked himself what he could do,
And then he found the answers.
He'd form a new ballet troop with
Exciting young black dancers.
He'd go uptown to Harlem
To find them and to reach them.
He'd build his own new school so he could
Train them there and teach them.

In the basement of a local church,
He started up his school.
His hardest job — convincing boys
That ballet could be cool.
'Cause ballet stars are athletes
Who train their bodies well,
Like players in the NBA
Or in the NFL.

It took him several years, but
Arthur Mitchell reached his goal,
Creating right in Harlem
What he calls "ballet with soul" —
A company that tours the world
And makes the critics sing.
It's Arthur Mitchell's tribute
To Martin Luther King.

MUHAMMAD ALI
1942
World heavyweight champion

Well, I float like a butterfly,
Sting like a bee –
World heavyweight champ,
Muhammad Ali.

Yeah, I'm the greatest.
I'm the best.
They want to put me
To the test –
Liston, Patterson,
Norton, Moore,
Quarry, Frazier,
And lots more.

In all the world,
In every city,
They're wild for me
'Cause I'm so pretty.
Won Golden Gloves,
Olympics, too.
In boxing, nothing
I can't do.

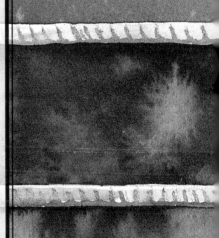

Right cross,
Left hook,
Uppercuts –
That's how I knock 'em
On their butts.
'Cause when they face me,
There's no hope.
I fool 'em with
My "rope-a-dope!"

'Cause I'm the greatest!
Yes, that's me –
World heavyweight champ,
Muhammad Ali.

World heavyweight champ,
Muhammad Ali
    POW!
    BAM!
    KNOCK OUT!

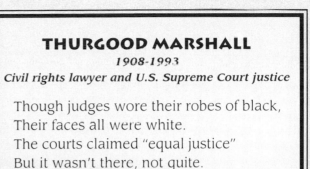

THURGOOD MARSHALL
1908-1993
Civil rights lawyer and U.S. Supreme Court justice

Though judges wore their robes of black,
Their faces all were white.
The courts claimed "equal justice"
But it wasn't there, not quite.

Supreme Court judges set the tone
For courts around the nation,
Where "equal justice" was for whites,
And blacks got segregation.

But Thurgood Marshall, lawyer for
The NAACP,
Said we must work within the courts
To get our victory.

He worked for years preparing suits
That fought discrimination
In schools, elections, restaurants,
And public transportation.

At last he won the case of "Brown"
That rewrote all the rules
And ended segregation
In our nation's public schools.

His brilliance now was recognized
By all across the nation,
And Lyndon Johnson gave him a
Supreme Court nomination.

For civil rights, a victory;
For bigotry, defeat.
Thurgood Marshall, first black man
To hold a high court seat.

GUION STEWART BLUFORD, JR.
1946
Astronaut

Guion Stewart Bluford, Jr.
      B.A.
      M.A.
      Ph.D.

      Studied math
      And laser physics,
      Aerospace technology.

Guion Stewart Bluford, Jr.
      Hero,
      Pilot,
      Wartime ace.

Guion Stewart Bluford, Jr.
      First black
      Man in
      Outer space.

MIRROR, MIRROR

Mirror, Mirror
On the wall,
Who will answer
Freedom's call?

Who will fight
In Freedom's ring,
Stained with blood
Of Reverend King?

The ring where
Medgar Evers fell,
Fighting till the
Final bell,
Where Malcolm X and
Rosa Parks,
Nelson Mandela,
Made their marks,

Where Douglass challenged
Slavery
In battles marked by
Bravery,
Determination,
Tears and pain,
Of lives destroyed
For selfish gain.

Here so many
Fought and died.
So many wept,
So many tried.
So many struggled
For so long
To live the dream,
To right the wrong.

But of the future,
What will be?
Who leads us now
To victory?

Tell us, Mirror,
Where to turn.
Who can teach us
How to learn
To live with
Justice, honor, truth,
Quell the violence,
Free the youth?

Who will show us
What is right,
Drive the hatred
From the night?

Who'll protect
The poor and weak?
The silent mirror
Does not speak.

And yet it holds
the answer true.
Look into it.
The answer — YOU !

ABOUT THE AUTHORS

Susan Altman and Susan Lechner, who both live in Washington, D.C., produce the Emmy Award-winning television programs "It's Academic," "It's Elementary," and "Pick Up the Beat." Ms. Altman, the producer, and Ms. Lechner, senior editor, have been involved in television since 1961 when "It's Academic" was created. Ms. Altman also is the author of the play, *Out of the Whirlwind*, and the book, *Extraordinary Black Americans from Colonial to Contemporary Times*.

ABOUT THE ARTIST

Byron Wooden, a free-lance illustrator and multi-media artist, was born and raised in San Diego, California, where he presently resides. His work has been exhibited in galleries and art shows throughout the United States. He has created ads for such corporations as Coca Cola, Embassy Suites Hotels, HomeFed Savings, and Sea World. He has received a First Place Award for Editorial Cartooning from the Journalism Association of Community Colleges and the Action Enterprises Black Achievement Award in the field of fine art. Most recently, *Artist Magazine* named him as a National Painting Competition Finalist.

ACKNOWLEDGMENTS

Project Editor: Alice Flanagan

Design and Electronic Page Composition: Beth Herman Design Associates

Engraver: Liberty Photoengravers

Printer: Lake Book Manufacturing, Inc.

Library of Congress Cataloging-in-Publication Data

Altman, Susan.
   Followers of the North Star : rhymes about African American heroes, heroines, and historical times / by Susan Altman and Susan Lechner : illustrated by Byron Wooden.
      p. cm.
   Summary: A collection of poems about some of the historical experiences of African Americans and about such prominent people as Benjamin Banneker, Matthew Henson, Rosa Parks, Jackie Robinson, and Leontyne Price.
   ISBN 0-516-05151-2
   1. Afro-Americans–Biography–Juvenile poetry.
2. Children's poetry, American. [1. Afro-American–Poetry. 2. American poetry–Collections.] I. Lechner, Susan. II. Wooden, Byron, ill. III. Title.
PS3551.L7943F6   1993
811'.54–dc20   93-797
                                                CIP
                                                AC